A Garden For You

SCOTT T. CRANE

WestBow Press books may be ordered through booksellers or by contacting:

WestBow Press
A Division of Thomas Nelson & Zondervan
1663 Liberty Drive
Bloomington, IN 47403
www.westbowpress.com
844-714-3454

Scripture quotations are from the New Revised Standard Version Bible, copyright © 1989 National Council of the Churches of Christ in the United States of America. Used by permission. All rights reserved worldwide.

ISBN: 978-1-6642-3139-9 (sc)
ISBN: 978-1-6642-3140-5 (e)

Library of Congress Control Number: 2021908135

Print information available on the last page.

WestBow Press rev. date: 05/19/2021

WESTBOW
P R E S S®
A DIVISION OF THOMAS NELSON
& ZONDERVAN

Author's note/Foreword to parents: it is not easy talking about death with children. The most we can do is simply be there with them in their sadness, not quite understanding fully the cycle of life. With a trusted adult there to console them, it becomes easier to let their tears fall down. In fact, there probably isn't much difference between what they need...and what we need ourselves. This story may produce tears; let them fall and simply be. Acknowledge the sadness, and share it with someone. Eventually, the shared grief becomes a shared strength. Additional resources for loss and grief are found at the end of the book.

"Peace I leave with you; my peace I give you. I do not give to you as the world gives. Do not let your hearts be troubled and do not be afraid." John 14:27

~ Rev. Dr. Scott T. Crane

I can't send you flowers anymore

So I guess I'll plant some seeds

I'll plant you a garden

Filled with the most beautiful plants of all

There would be fronds of ferns

Towers of trees

Flowers of all kinds and colors

And rocks with soft moss

There would be burbling streams

And falling waters

And mountains with snow

There would be valleys of wildflowers

Where animals roam free

And, just for you, I would plant

An especially special seed

The seed would sprout and grow

Growing taller and Taller and TALLER!

Until it reached the clouds

And then it would grow all the way up into heaven

You could climb it whenever you wanted

You and the Angels could visit like old friends

And then, if you wanted, could
you come and visit me?

I miss you.

So I will plant some seeds that say I love you

And even when you are so far away
I cannot reach you anymore

There will still be a spot of color to
remind me that I loved you

And you loved me.

~ stc

Additional Resources

For walking through the grieving process, parents and other caring adults should review texts for compatibility with their particular spiritual journey, and for compatibility with the journey of your child. Some of these texts fit older pilgrims on grief's journey, and others are directed toward those who offer help to children who grieve.

1. The Dougy Center: The National Center for Grieving Children and Families offers many resources and can be contacted here: https://www.dougy.org/. 503-775-5683. Or by mail: PO Box 86852 Portland, OR 97286.
2. *What About the Kids? Understanding Their Needs in Funeral Planning & Services* (Portland, OR: The Dougy Center for Grieving Children, 1999).
3. Haugk, Kenneth C. *Journeying Through Grief: A Time To Grieve* (St. Louis, Missouri: Stephen Ministries, 2004, 2019)
4. Haugk, Kenneth C. *Journeying Through Grief: Experiencing Grief* (St. Louis, Missouri: Stephen Ministries, 2004, 2019)
5. Haugk, Kenneth C. *Journeying Through Grief: Finding Hope And Healing* (St. Louis, Missouri: Stephen Ministries, 2004, 2019)
6. Haugk, Kenneth C. *Journeying Through Grief: Rebuilding And Remembering* (St. Louis, Missouri: Stephen Ministries, 2004, 2019)
7. Lester, Andrew D. *Pastoral Care with Children in Crisis* (Louisville, KY: Westminster John Knox Pres, 1985.

8. Grossoehme, Daniel H., and Harold G. Koenig. *The Pastoral Care of Children* (Philadelphia, PA: Routledge, Taylor & Francis Group, 1999).

9. Garrett, Greg. *Stories from the Edge: A Theology of Grief* (Philadelphia, PA: Westminster John Knox Press, 2008).

10. Reeves, Nancy. *A Path Through Loss: A Workbook for Healing and Growth – Updated and Expanded* (Philadelphia, PA: Westminster John Knox Press, 2012).